JOURNAL *of* TRAVEL ACROSS THE PLAINS
TO CALIFORNIA AND GUIDE TO THE
FUTURE EMIGRANT

JOURNAL *of* TRAVEL ACROSS THE PLAINS TO CALIFORNIA AND GUIDE TO THE FUTURE EMIGRANT

Dr. JAMES S. SHEPHERD

YE GALLEON PRESS

FAIRFIELD, WASHINGTON

1978

Library of Congress Cataloging in Publication Data

Shepherd, James S.
    Journal of travel across the Plains to California and guide to
the future emigrant.

    First published in 1851.
    Running title: Across the Plains to California.
    Includes index.
    1. Overland journeys to the Pacific. 2. Shepherd, James S.
3. Pioneers--The West--Biography. 4. The West--Biography.
I. Title.
F593.S54   1978   917.8'04'2   78-10783
ISBN 0-87770-170-9

INTRODUCTION

The James S. Shepherd overland to California is one of the rarest known items of western U.S. history. Bibliographies mention a copy in the Rollins Library, Princeton University, which copy has since disappeared. There was however at least one other original copy held by Mr. George Langlois, a California printer. In correspondence he mentions this copy and states that he was offered 425 dollars for it, a price presumably well under its true value even several decades ago. Mr. Langlois printed or had printed a very neat reprint in 1945, pp. ii, 45, presumably Placerville, California, in an edition of 200 copies. At least some of the copies came into possession of Emil J. Bergmann, an antiquarian book dealer located in Brooklyn, N.Y.

Bibliographies list the author as Joseph S. Shepherd, apparently an error as no such person appears in any early city directories of Racine, Wisconsin. A James S. Shepherd, M.D. is listed in the *Racine Register Business Directory of 1850*, with an address of 164 Wisconsin. Again in *The Racine City Directory 1858* James S. Shepherd, M.D. is listed with an address of Main & 5th.

A letter was written by George Langlois to the Mayor of Racine, dated December 15, 1944, and giving an address of Route 2, Placerville, California, at which time Mr. Langlois represented his age to be ninety. The letter states that Dr. James S. Shepherd lived in Racine from May 26, 1856 to March 31, 1906. If this information is correct then James S. Shepherd had returned from California by that date. The *Journal* states that on August 15, 1850 he began the practice of Medicine with Dr. Ruddock, in Placerville. The *Journal* is represented to have been published by Mrs. Rebecca Shepherd at Racine in 1851, so apparently Dr. Shepherd mailed the hand written material back to his wife who had it published.

It is possible that the original copy that Mr. George Langlois worked from may still be in existence but its location is unknown. Efforts to trace descendents of James S. Shepherd have been unsuccessful. Relatives of

INTRODUCTION

James S. Shepherd lived at 12th and South Main in Racine, but present occupants of this address have no knowledge of James S. Shepherd.

Presumably a number of copies must still exist of the little paper bound booklet printed by or for George Langlois in 1945. An edition of 200 copies is very small and as a number of surviving copies are presumably locked up in libraries the 1945 reprint of James S. Shepherd is an item that only rarely turns up in the antiquarian book market.

The back cover of the Placerville reprint, and presumably of the 1851 Racine original, carries an advertisement from a "Mark Miller, Bookseller and Publisher, Sign of the Rag Man." He wants to buy 500 tons of rags, leading one to speculate that unsold copies of the 1851 original edition of Dr. Shepherd's book may have been pulped, or they may have been destroyed by fire, the fate of a number of rare titles of western U.S. history that were printed in small printing offices.

INTRODUCTION

In preparing the succeeding pages for publication, (according to promise,) my object has not been so much to form an elaborate work, as a faithful account of our travels and vicissitudes, which will, and must always, to a certain extent, arise in a journey of three thousand miles over land, the greater part being through a savage, hostile and barren country, full of mountains, the extent of which no one can have the least conception of, who has not passed over this same route. If any errors occur, and doubtless there are many, I hope my friends will impute them rather to incompetency than design, as I have been all along determined to adhere to facts as closely as possible, even when they were anything but agreeable to disclose. I have also endeavored to make the journal as complete a guide as possible for the future Emigrant, if there should be any bold enough to undertake it. A man may be excused for trying it once; but he that passed over such an inhospitable country a second time, can scarcely be considered to be in his proper senses. I am aware that my distances do not in all cases agree with some previous estimates, but they have all forgot to include the going to, and returning from camping grounds, which must be done by all who travel on such a road, and belong as much to the journey as passing round any obstruction which you cannot get over. I have submitted it occasionally to different members of our party, and they have in every instance considered it as complete as possible; and acting upon their decision, I send it, greeting amongst my old neighbors, hoping that they may, in some measure, be both instructed and amused.

J. S. Shepherd

Across the Plains to California

WE started from Racine, Wisconsin, March 5th, 1850, in company with Barton, Bennet, Fleming, Lytle, Hamilton, Pugh, Van Cott, D. and S. Richardson, Waldron, Rice, Martindale, Pearsons, Cornell, Van Horn, Dickinson, and Utley. Passed through Wisconsin to Galena, without anything remarkable occurring, unloaded all our heavy goods, and shipped them from thence round by St. Louis to St. Joseph, the boats not being able to proceed up the Missouri River as far as Council Bluffs, on account of the scarcity of water. We made a great mistake in buying part of our outfit at St. Louis, everything being at St. Joseph that is necessary for the journey at comparatively low prices; whereas, we had to pay forty cents per hundred to get them there. A great deal could also have been saved by buying everything there, and starting from home with empty wagons; and one thing must be held in remembrance by all who come after us, viz: that the first of April is soon enough to leave the Lake shore, or they will have to undergo the mortification of laying by here on the frontier four weeks at least, as we have done, and I can safely say, it is the dullest work that ever was undertaken by man, to say nothing of the discouraging effect it has on the spirits, and I do believe it is the main reason why so many turn back. On leaving Galena we struck the Mississippi River, eight miles below, and not being able to ferry over that evening, the wagon I travelled in had our first insight at camping on its broad banks. The night was fine, and we got along very comfortably. Mr. Smith, the ferryman, rowed us over early next morning, and we caught up before the other teams started. There is nothing particularly worthy of note in passing through Iowa, unless it is, that as a State, as far as we could judge, it is far behind Wisconsin. There are very poor accommodations for travellers, and the farther you go West, the worse you find it. Bloomfield is the last village you pass through in Iowa, and soon after cross the line into Missouri; and then you not only see, but feel the blighting effects of the Peculiar Institution; for I have no hesitation in saying that Missouri, or at least part of it through which we passed, is a century behind Wisconsin, we saw nothing but log cabins, not even in their county towns, and those of the most slovenly and worst description. As to the inhabitants, you will see them (I had almost said all of them) lounging about the miserable places called villages, with saddle horses tied in every direction; for they all ride on horseback, and every little petty groggery you enter you will find a few choice specimens, playing at cards; consequently it is a difficult thing to see a farmer, on your whole route through the State, who has got more than one corn patch cleared up, and that, generally a very small one. I understand things are something better in the Southern part of the State. We arrived at St. Joseph, April 1st. It is a thriving town of about two thousand inhabitants, and but seven years old. Its prosperity is, I believe, mainly owing to the California emigration. One of our party, S. Richardson, here left us and returned home. We found feed for horses scarce and dear, (no wonder, in such a lazy country,) and after staying there three weeks, and the last one without a mouthful of hay, we struck our camp and removed to Weston, twenty-eight miles down the river, a pretty and thriving town, and encamped there, but after investigation, crossed the river on Wednesday, April 24th, and encamped within a half a mile of Fort Leavenworth, where we obtained a ton of hay, and where there is a tolerable supply of grass, at least enough for our horses to commence upon.

Fort Leavenworth is beautifully situated on the south side of the river in the Indian territory, is pretty well built, and has altogether a picturesque appearance. There are about three hundred soldiers stationed here at present; but some are going to other forts in the interior this spring. There are also a number of teamsters, and wagons, and mules, this being the point where Uncle Sam collects his horses together, preparatory to going as supplies over land to several other stations. After passing several days comfortably enough, compared with the quarters we had left, we loaded a spare wagon procured for the purpose, with thirteen hundred of hay, and on

May 1st

Struck our tents (by-the-by, an important article and absolutely indispensable for each wagon) and made a start, leaving the frontier of civilization behind us. After travelling five miles we encamped on Salt creek, to endeavor to get Fratt's company, who were lying in the neighborhood, to join us; but they were not inclined to start until Monday, the 6th, so we concluded by a vote of the company to go without them, and on the

May 2nd

Proceeded; made fifteen miles to-day, greater part of the way being through a rain storm which continued all night, and delayed us till nine o'clock in the morning of

May 3rd

Weather fair; were joined this evening by four wagons and nine men from Missouri; made twenty miles.

May 4th

Proceeded with nine wagons and twenty-seven men in our train. Weather cold and grass scarce; made twenty miles.

May 5th

In measuring a mile, and timing it several times since we started, I find our general travel to be three miles per hour; made twenty-two miles.

May 6th

Grass continues scarce; we find our hay very useful; made twenty-four miles.

James S. Shepherd

May 7th

Rainy morning; started at ten o'clock, and after travelling sixteen miles, struck the high road from St. Joe West, one hundred and twenty miles. From Fort Leavenworth, the road we have travelled, is a new one made by Uncle Sam's men this spring, and is better than any road leading from Racine, not excepting even the Plank; but we were told it was at least sixty or seventy miles nearer new Fort Kearney, (or Fort Childs, as it is sometimes called,) than any other starting point on the Missouri River, which is not the case; for where the roads join, by comparing notes with travellers on the route, I find we differ two miles and that in favor of St. Joe, their reckoning being one hundred and twenty, and mine one hundred and twenty-two. We have now a road before us, which appears to be travlled on as much as if the country had been for fifty years in the highest state of civilization; made sixteen miles.

May 8th

Our rate of travelling not being fast enough for some of our new Missouri friends, three wagons of them left us this evening; but we expect to overhaul them before long, feed being scarce at present, and consequently not the time to try our teams; made twenty-four miles.

May 9th

Found better feed than we expected, so laid over today, and counted one hundred and ninety-five wagons that passed on the road close by; most of them with little or no dry feed; guess they will have to lie by soon; our dry feed in the shape of kiln-dried Indian meal will last about ten days longer.

May 10th

Struck our camp to-day at half past 6 o'clock; in one mile forded the Big Blue River, a fine clear stream, four rods wide, and two feet deep. To-day, for want of wood and water, we travelled thirty miles and passed sixty-six wagons. Frosty nights and sunny days; not much prospect of grass; made thirty miles.

May 11th

Fine warm day; made sixteen miles.

May 12th

Sunday; weather hot; but no convenience for laying over; made eighteen miles.

May 13th

We are now encamped on the Little Blue, a beautiful stream about eighty miles from the Big Blue. We have met several emigrants returning on account of the scarcity of grass; but still they are coming by hundreds every day. We are getting into the Buffalo region, some having been seen to-day; hope soon to have some fresh beef; to-day has been quite hot, and the ground is parched up so that grass cannot grow. Rain would indeed be a blessing. Two of our horses were lost to-night, and two men lost in seeking for them; made fifteen miles.

May 14th

The horses are found this morning and the men also; one of them (Hugh Pugh) having wandered over the prairie all night; the other availed himself of the hospitality of a neighboring camp. Our route continues along the valley of the Little Blue; made sixteen miles.

May 15th

The road continues along the river valley; made fifteen miles.

May 16th

Today, after travelling fourteen miles, we took in wood and water, and left the river valley. The weather is hot and dry, no rain having yet fallen, and we have to use considerable discretion in choosing our camping grounds, as feed is excessively scarce, and our horses easily worn out if we do not manage well; made seventeen miles.

May 17th

This morning, for the same reason as mentioned before, our other Missouri friends left us, but we had the gratification of passing them before night;

for want of wood and water, we travelled thirty miles and reached the Platte. The country between the Missouri and Platte Rivers is one immense Prairie, intersected (on the route we travelled) by the Big and Little Blue Rivers, and a number of creeks (generally at distances proper for camping places for travellers) which supply both wood and water, a few scattering Cotton-wood trees being along the courses of them all; and that is all the timber the country affords. The soil is generally good, but requires more rain than has fallen this spring. It has at present a rather barren appearance, and the difficulty of obtaining grass for our horses barely to subsist upon has been great. We have already seen some dead horses, mules and oxen, and thirteen human graves, but the graves are all of previous seasons. I think at present there has been but little sickness; we have heard of cholera, but we hear a great many reports without foundation. We have not seen an Indian since leaving Fort Leavenworth, but hear of them and their depredations continually, but do not believe them. It will be observed, in my daily report, that on the 14th, 15th, and 16th, our course was along the valley of the Little Blue, forty-five miles; it then leaves it without crossing, and strikes off to the Platte, thirty-three miles. Water, sufficient for cooking purposes, should be taken from the Little Blue, and wood can be had eight or ten miles further on; but there are more than twenty miles without either. The Platte is a wide, shallow stream, water muddy, current swift, grass scarce and weather dry. The road, so far, has been as good as can be on the face of the earth; made thirty miles.

May 18th

Laid over to-day; found good grass on Grand Island, in the river, forty-five miles long. Fort Kearney is situated opposite its head, and is eleven miles from our camp. We were joined tonight by three wagons from Janesville, Wisconsin, and ten men.

May 19th

Sunday. Struck camp and travelled to the Fort; posted our letters—mail leaves on the 21st for the States. Traded some dried peaches and loaf sugar for a far more indispensable article, viz: flour—175 lb.; and after going three miles further, encamped. The next point is Fort Laramie—distance, three hundred and thirty-seven miles, as they tell us. There have been two thousand three hundred wagons passed Fort Kearney before us; but the grass is improving, and instead of forcing our horses, they are all in fine condition, and we are decidedly after them, and expect to pass two-thirds of them in a month. We have begun the use of the "Bois de Vache" or Buffalo chips for fuel—it is an excellent substitute for wood; made fourteen miles.

May 20th

Had a thunder storm last night, attended with a very welcome shower of rain, which makes everything look green and cheerful; roads good, grass tolerable; made twenty-eight miles.

May 21st

Fine grass weather—soon have plenty of feed; we were joined to-day by one wagon and three men from Michigan City, Indiana. Roads good as can be; made twenty-five miles.

May 22nd

High winds this evening, which blew the tent over after we were in bed, much to our discomfort, but luckily unattended with rain, so that after a hearty laugh all was soon put to rights. We were joined to-day by one wagon and three men from Peoria, Illinois. Feed good; made twenty-two miles.

May 23rd

Were overtaken to-day by three wagons from Racine, Dickinson, Schobey & Co., whom we passed on the Little Blue, lying by for repairs. On account of our company being already large for the amount of feed to be found in any one place, they declined to fall in, preferring sooner to travel alone than subject the horses to a scarcity of feed. They are also afraid we travel too slow for them.. We are now encamped near the forks of the Platte, one hundred miles from Fort Kearney, and are progressing well and safely, our horses being in better condition than when we left home, although we have had no grain for them since we left the last fort; we made as gradual a change as possible, therefore they do not seem to miss it; but, I am fully persuaded that we ought to have grain, particularly for horses, the first thousand miles; it will then be late enough for the grass to have attained some strength; made twenty-five miles.

May 24th

Roads good, and after having the best grass we have seen, started at half-past six o'clock, and drove to where the road leaves the river, twenty-five miles from the Forks. Here we found several teams fording, but we declined and took the road which leads off to the left hand, and crossed the bluffs. After a drive of five miles we came again to the river valley and encamped. Grass tolerable. One of our men, (Mr. Fleming,) who has been out all day with his gun, has just come in loaded with Buffalo beef, as tired as can be—hunting on foot and following the wagons, being anything but a joke, in a hot day, particularly when they are successful, the game being very burdensome. He also killed a Hare and an Antelope, which he was obliged to leave. To-morrow morning we breakfast for the first time on the famous Buffalo beef; made thirty miles.

May 25th

Our breakfast was indeed a treat—the meat being delicious, especially after having had nothing but salt provisions for so long. We encamped to-night at four o'clock, for the express purpose of having a buffalo hunt. Our camp was suddenly turned into a scene of excitement, while we were busy cooking our supper on the banks of the Platte, the cry was, "a buffalo is crossing the river close by." Operations were immediately abandoned—some rushed for guns, and others for horses; at length, as he arrived on our side, several footmen were there to receive him, as also several horseman were scattering themselves over the prairie, should it be necessary to give him chase. But one shot was fired as he landed, which was ineffectual, and away he bounded over the plain, riders with their arms in order after him in good earnest, but in spite of all their efforts, he at first gained on them considerably. I had volunteered to stay and attend camp, so stood a spectator and enjoyed the fun. After a five or six mile run they succeeded in killing him — the gun of John Lytle bringing him down. A wagon was sent from camp, and the best parts, to the amount of at least 500 pounds, brought in; so now we can feast indeed. Whilst the above was going on the most terrific gale suddenly passed over I have ever seen. Tents were blown down and torn to pieces; wagon covers shared the same fate, and hats &c. were lost — but a calm has succeeded, and all is still; made twenty miles.

May 26th

Sunday. Laid over to rest and feast, as well as to attend to other small duties, such as washing, &c.

Pulled up stakes and off; after going twenty-five miles, we came to the ford of the Platte, where the river is half a mile wide and averaging two and a half feet deep, current strong and swift. We crossed without disaster, which some failed to do, and after going about two miles up the north side for grass, encamped, with at least five hundred wagons in sight, the majority of them horse teams; made twenty-seven miles.

May 28th

Got an early start, hoping to leave some if not all of the crowd behind, and succeeded — being the first on the road. After fifteen miles travel over a barren plain, nearly destitute of vegetation, came suddenly upon Ash Hollow, (so called, I suppose, from a number of ash trees which grow there, and are a welcome object to the eye of the traveller weary with everlasting prairie,) and a splendid scene presented itself; ridges of rock, and deep defiles, some rugged and frowning, whilst others are covered partially with cedar, occasionally intermingled with the wild cherry in full bloom. The road leads through the hollow five or six miles, and I rather fancy we had a slight specimen of mountain travelling; however, since we all got safely through, and striking the North Fort of the Platte, travelled some distance up its valley, and passing some romantic scenery, at last came to a good place to camp, in the immediate neighborhood of Indians, several of whom soon after, paid us a visit. They are friendly, and appear to be a very fine race, and as we are now in their territory it is best to be on good terms, but I believe the "Sioux" have always been so with the "Pale Faces;" made twenty-eight miles.

May 29th

Last night we had a fine rain, which is cheering, grass being hard to meet with. We have passed close by five encampments of Indians to-day, and find them to be most intolerably urgent beggars. Some of our company have traded with them for moccasins, &c. They are rather good looking, (the countenance being mild and placid,) tolerably clean. On account of not being able to stop sooner, for want of grass, we drove thirty miles.

May 30th

We have had the Court House Rock in sight the greater part of the day; it is a strangely isolated mass, resembling remarkably an architectural structure, as well as a smaller one close by, which, from the road, strikingly reminds the beholder of a low country church; made twenty miles.

May 31st

We supposed we were encamped last night near the Court House; but after an hour and a half drive, this morning, found ourselves opposite to it, but nearly as far off as ever; so none of us visited it, much to our chagrin. But Chimney Rock has been sometime in sight and is said to be but sixteen miles off; so we determined to drive near it and then turn out to noon. We drove to within fifteen miles of it, and the Rock appearing close to us, as soon as we had dinner, off some of us started, expecting about a two mile walk; but there are deceptions on the Plains as well as in civilized society, and distance is decidedly one of them, for after an hour and a half smart walking, we found ourselves still in the distance; but, however, we at last reached it and were amply remunerated. An accurate description will be difficult, but I will try. There can be no doubt but it has been a high mound of earth, much higher than the top of the Chimney now is, as it is fast wearing away by the action of storms, which have been the agents that have reduced it to its present singular form. The principal material of which it is composed, is a species of marl, which in cutting out my name reminded me exceedingly of dried unburnt brick, such as are made in Racine, and it also, after wetting, splits in pieces in drying in the same manner, consequently continues to wear away; and the same cause continuing to act, must ere long destroy its beauty. Its present shape is a half globe inverted, with irregular surfaces, and a column rising out of the centre; the whole being about two hundred and fifty feet high. It has a vein of limestone rock running through the centre on a plain level, which shows, conclusively, that its present state is not owing to any convulsion of nature. Fremont, I believe, says that when first discovered, it was five hundred feet in height. There are many other curious bluffs in the neighborhood, all of the same material, and consequently assume a variety of shapes by the action of the above named causes. We made to-day twenty-six miles.

June 1st

Nineteen miles from Chimney Rock, (or Chimney Mound, as it ought to be called,) are Scott's Bluffs, so called, I believe, from a trapper of that name being left at their base, (unable, through sickness, to proceed any further) not by the savage Indian, but by his remorseless companions, calling themselves civilized men. About six miles before you come to the bluffs

(the road leaves the river; here it is necessary to take in water, as you pass through a valley, between two mountain ranges, for twenty miles without a drop. As you pass over the hills, at the end of the valley, you strike a creek with several beautiful springs of pure cold water. Close against our camp, from a high bluff, we obtained a splendid view of the Laramie Peak of the Rocky Mountains; made twenty-eight miles.

June 2nd

Sunday. For want of grass, we were obliged to leave camp; so moved on to Horse Creek and there laid over; made ten miles.

June 3rd

Our horses having had good grass, we made an early start, and after about twelve miles again came to the river; made twenty-six miles.

June 4th

To-day, ten miles drive brought us to Fort Laramie. We had to raise our wagon-boxes in order to ford Laramie Fork, one mile before reaching the Fort. We posted our letters and spent some little time in looking around. There are at present about one hundred soldiers stationed here. The fort stands upon a beautiful site; but, as yet, there is not much improvement made. We proceeded and encamped outside the boundaries of Uncle Sam; making, in all, thirteen miles.

June 5th

Some of us appear rather differently, having taken off our wagon covers, and shortened our wagons as much as possible, the road being now, for the most part, hilly. About five miles from the Fort, we came to the Black Hills, which continue fifty or sixty miles. Here we find a full supply of good wood, water, and grass for camping purposes—far better than we have yet met with. We are encamped to-night, on a small mountain stream, with the Rocky Mountains in full view; made twenty-six miles.

Across the Plains to California

June 6th

The country is generally studded with dwarf pines, and the scenery romantic, with an occasional touch of the beautiful. Feed and water tolerable; made twenty-four miles.

June 7th

A division in the camp—probably through mistake, and may be only temporary—but the wagon I am in, and two others, are ahead. We are now decidedly amongst the mountains, and rather guess are taking a preparatory glimpse of the elephant. Feed and water rather scarce; made twenty-seven miles.

June 8th

Plenty of good running water—grass scarce. This evening our wagon and one of the others returned to the original crowd, the other driving on and leaving us behind. By going about two miles from the road, up stream, we found good feed for our horses. It being Saturday, and we all anxious for a day of rest; made seventeen miles.

June 9th

Sunday. Laid over, on the banks of the Fourche de Bois River, a swift mountain stream—water good.

June 10th

Struck camp early, and in four miles came again to the Platte, which we had not seen since leaving Fort Laramie. The road now follows the river until it crosses the ferry. There is no scarcity of water, but grass is out of the question. Our horses would barely subsist without working; and the great difficulty of the route to California, seems to be a scarcity of food for teams; made twenty-six miles.

June 11th

A drive of fifteen miles brought us to the Ferry, which, instead of being a lonely place in the wilderness, appears to be a bustling market town. There are six boats on the river going all the time. It takes about ten minutes to cross and back—and at least five hundred wagons have gone over to-day, with the prospect of continuing at the same rate for some time to come. The charge is four dollars per wagon, and twenty-five cents per horse. After getting safely over, we proceeded, and encamped on the plains, where there is not grass enough on an acre to keep a sheep from starvation. We had also to fill our casks at the river, there being no good water in twenty-six miles; made seventeen miles.

June 12th

We are now in a part of the country, the road through which needs a more particular description, there being several dangerous points to be avoided, and which, to be shunned need only to be pointed out correctly. Twelve miles from the Ferry there is a mineral spring and lake, which, when undisturbed, is clear and good, but when stirred, in the least, turns black, and becomes a deadly poison. All the water you come to within twenty-four miles is equally dangerous—numbers of skeletons being scattered around as evidence of its baneful character. In twenty miles the road passes through a fissure in the rocks for about a quarter of a mile, in passing through which, we obtained a splendid view of the South Pass, but it was almost immediately hidden from sight amongst the hills through which we are wending our way. In twenty-six miles we came to a small creek, on the left, which is tolerable water—at least it is safe to use. The road passes along side of it about a quarter of a mile. Two miles further on, there is Willow Spring, said to be a splendid place to encamp. The water certainly is good but the grass—about the same as Main-street, Racine. The horses have been taken about four miles over the hills, in quest of feed, but now, as I am writing, have come in as hungry as when they left; made twenty-six miles.

June 13th

Contrary to our expectations, some scouts that were out, found a small but good patch of grass; so we concluded to stay and let our horses eat it up, which, after being done, we started as late as half-past four o'clock, and went twelve miles. No lack of good water. We encamped by a small creek, some distance from the road, on the left hand. All our party, except the three wagons that left Racine together, on the fifth of March, left us to-day, our rate of travel being too slow; made twelve miles.

June 14th

Left camp early, and after fifteen miles, well watered, struck the Sweet Water River, one mile below Independence Rock, an immense pile of isolated granite, close by the river, merely allowing space between for the road to pass. The Rock, (which in fact, is the commencement of the Rocky Mountains,) is literally covered with the names of travellers. One mile above, we forded the river, and passed up its valley on the west side, nine miles, and encamped close by the Devil's Gate, a singular fissure, through which the Sweet Water passes—the walls of granite rock rising perpendicularly, on either side, to the height of four hundred feet. Mr. Fleming and myself left the road, and went to examine this natural curiosity, and in attempting to pass through became strangely deceived, and had to climb over the rock twice—a dangerous task as well as difficult, and one that I would not again undertake for half my stake in California, and would earnestly advise others not to try it; made twenty-four miles.

June 15th

Found good grass, so concluded to lay over and keep Sabbath with the Hebrews.

June 16th

Sunday. Road has been heavy sand for the last fifty miles. To-day we have been wending our way with the rocky mountains on both sides, and they are very properly named, being immense piles of naked granite.) As we pass up the valley of the Sweet Water, in some places the snow is even down to the base, and consequently the weather is not very warm; made twenty-two miles.

June 17th

Road heavy sand, and travelling exceedingly hard. We still continue along the valley of the Sweet Water for fourteen miles. The road then turns to the left, around high bluffs of naked rock, and returns to the river again in eight miles; made twenty-two miles.

June 18th

The road here leaves the river for twenty-one miles, so we took in water, as good water does not occur in the whole distance. We struck at a ford, and in half a mile further forded a branch of it, and the road being good all day, made twenty-four miles.

June 19th

The road ascends for a mile, and then abruptly descending again strikes the river; and after fording twice, continues along the valley nine miles, crossing a number of creeks in its course. We accidentally heard of good grass two miles distant, over the bluffs, across the river, so encamped; and sending the horses over, with a guard, laid by the rest of the day, having made but ten milles.

June 20th

We now leave the river and ascend the bluffs, turning to the right. In three miles some rough, rocky ridges occur, which are dangerous to wagons, if great care is not used. We, however, all passed over safely. We saw a new made grave to-day, and on the head-board, the following inscription: *To the memory of Columbus, who was found with his throat cut, and in his hand a pocket knife with a death grip, June 19, 1850. May he rest in peace.* The persons who had found and buried him left a statement the following day, with the Express Mail Line Post Office, at Pacific Springs, that every clue to his identity appeared to have been destroyed. A Lieutenant's commission in the U.S. Army was in his pocket, with the names all torn off. There can be no doubt but he was on foot, and alone—got tired and disheartened, and committed suicide to put an end to his journey over the mountains. The road is good, but hilly, with no lack of water; it strikes the river again and fords it in twenty-two miles for the last time. The next stream we meet with will run the same way we are going, or toward the Pacific Ocean; made twenty-two miles.

Across the Plains to California

June 21st

After a drive of seven miles we passed between the Twin Mounds, the last particular objects on the road East of the Rocky Mountains. Three miles beyond is the South Pass, or summit of the ridge. We then begin to descend, and are nearly one thousand miles from the Missouri River, or where we began to ascend. The largest half of the journey from the Frontier to the Diggings is now undoubtedly accomplished. (Note.—The author has since learned, to his cost, that the above statement is erroneous; and, that instead of the largest half, but little more than one-third of the route lies East of the South Pass.) Three miles further brought us to Pacific Creek and Springs. This is the first water we have seen running the same way we are travelling. Here is the last opportunity that presents itself to the traveller to send home. Some of us availed ourselves of it. There is no water that can be depended on as good at all times, for twenty-five miles; so, filling our casks, we proceeded over a fine road for some distance, and encamped, for the first time on the Western slope—grass scarce; made twenty-three miles.

June 22nd

A drive of half a mile brought us to the Dry Sandy. There is some little water, said not to be good, but I believe it is not hurtful—at all events it is used by some. Eight miles further, the road forks—the left hand going to Fort Bridges and the Mormon settlement at Salt Lake—(it is also the old Fort Hall road)—the right, or rather straight ahead, is Sublett's Cut Off. Some of the emigration takes the left hand via the Salt Lake, but the majority the Cut Off. Four miles further is Little Sandy—a good stream of good water. Another drive of six miles brought us to the Big Sandy and confines of our first desert. Here it is usual to stay a little time to rest and feed, there being before us a drive of thirty-five miles without grass of a drop of water. Three miles from camp we found pretty good grass, so took our horses thither, and shall remain in camp till about three o'clock, to-morrow, when we shall commence our weary way across, and expect, by driving all night to arrive at Green River early in the morning; made eighteen miles.

June 23rd

Sunday. There is beginning to be considerable sickness, for some days, three or four of our men have been quite down. I had to wade through the river this morning and back again, (the horses being three miles off,) to visit the sick in other camps. The prevailing disease is camp, or rheumatic, called here Mountain Fever, which is a very appropriate appellation. At four o'clock, P.M., we forded the river, and commenced rolling along through what has been called a desert; but, to our great surprise, we found grass in some places, even more plentiful than it had been over a great deal of the country which we had passed. It is true, it is entirely deserted by streams of water, but with our large casks each holding forty gallons, we might have started early in the morning, and gone as far as possible through the day, and encamped over night, finishing the distance next morning with ease; and, I think it would have been quite as well for our horses, and much better for ourselves. As it was, we got safely over, and saw but five or six dead horses and oxen. We were led to believe it was only thirty-five miles, by a Guide Book, published by one Ware, of St. Louis, (which, by-the-by, in no single instance, that I have noticed, has it done anything but deceive,) thus making the last fifteen miles a dead weight on our hands; but let no one who reads this and ever crosses that plain, start without being prepared to go full fifty miles without water. We were twenty-one hours in crossing, (from four o'clock to ten,) then rested two hours, and fed some grass which we had with us, from twelve to four, and from six till one o'clock, making in all seventeen hours travel and some of it very fast. The road for fifteen miles at the further end, is very hilly and hard to get over; the remainder is good. We ferried over Green River, at Middle Ferry, which cost us five dollars per wagon, and had to swim our horses. Made, on the 23d and 24th, fifty miles.

June 25th

The grass on the River being all eaten up, we struck our camp, and passing over a very hilly road for twelve miles—came to a branch of Green River, grass being tolerable, we encamped; made twelve miles.

Across the Plains to California

This morning we moved again, feed not being good enough to lay by on. After following the valley of the Branch five miles, we struck across the Bluffs, and in ten miles more came to Cedar Grove, where we turned out two hours, for rest—not feed, there being nothing to feed on. There is no lack of water, creeks and springs being abundant. The road next ascends a long hill, and when on the top, we saw snow two hundred feet beneath us. We now began to descend, and continued for at least one thousand feet, where there is a creek at the bottom. We continued along two miles where there is a creek at the bottom. We continued along two miles further—water all the way—and encamped. To-day, we overtook one of the wagons which left us at Willow Springs; and they wishing to travel with us again, are doing so. One of them has been quite sick ever since they left us; made twenty-two miles.

June 27th

Got an early start, and travelled twelve miles, to Ham's Fork, a swift and deep stream. We had to raise our wagon beds six inches in order to keep our provisions, &c., dry. We stayed in the valley three hours to feed, with a Snake Indian encampment close by. One of our men (Bennet) traded horses with them. The road leaves the valley by ascending one of the longest and highest hills we have yet met with. At the top, a comparatively level Plain presents itself to the eye, over which we travelled some miles through a good grazing country, although surrounded on all sides by snow-capped mountains. No lack of water to-day. We encamped by a large grove of Poplars, where the mosquitoes almost ate us up, having made 22 miles.

June 28th

A drive of ten miles brought us to the Bear River Valley, over a very hilly road, into which we descended by quite a dangerous place. It was really astonishing that we all got down safely. We then passed along the valley twelve miles, and came to Smith's Fork. The road here turns suddenly to the right, between two mountains, and passing through the gorge, fords four times and returns to the other side of the stream, through the same gorge to the valley. We encamped three miles further on, in a bend of the river—grass good; made twenty-five miles.

June 29th

The road to-day continues along the river valley eighteen miles through the best grazing country we have seen. It then passes over the mountains ten miles, and again strikes Bear River. We came up to, and forded Thomas's Fork, sixteen miles from our morning's encampment; made twenty-eight miles.

June 30th

Laid in camp to-day to rest ourselves and horses; but it proved anything but a day of rest to me—a messenger arriving early from Fratt & Coil's camp, (back fifteen miles), announcing that Coil was very sick and wished to see me. Consequently I had to retrace fifteen miles of our hardest road, but found him somewhat relieved, and stayed with them that night.

July 1st

We started early, in order to overtake our train, Fratt & Co. being anxious to join us, which our wagons expecting, moved slowly, so that we came up at noon; and, after twelve miles further drive, encamped on a beautiful creek of excellent water—grass plenty. There are now eight wagons and twenty-nine men with us—train large enough. The road to-day continues along the river valley, crossing several beautiful but small mountain creeks. On account of delay, we made to-day only twelve miles.

July 2nd

Started early, and continuing along the valley, with plenty of water and grass, encamped at the finest spring that can be imagined. It is in fact a river, coming out of the rock, with plenty of the purest water to drive twenty run of stone. There is a great deal of sickness on the route—chiefly fevers. One of our men (Hugh Paul) is very sick indeed with Purpura Hon-oragica [*sic. purpura hemorrhagic*—black measles]; made thirty-two miles.

Across the Plains to California

July 3rd

One mile from our encampment we came to Beer, Soda, and Steamboat Springs, each one, itself, (but especially the Steamboat Spring,) is a curiosity well worth the attention of the traveller. Beer Spring water has to me, quite as agreeable a taste as the best Soda water made artificially, and would, I am well persuaded, be a handsome fortune for any one, could it be conveyed to some populous place. Some of our boys attempted to confine it in their canteens, but found it impossible — so restless is its nature, that the corks would not hold it. Steamboat Spring, to the left of the road, in a bend in the river, immediately on its brink, boils two or three feet out of the centre of a tabular rock, and makes a sound something similar to the puffing of a high pressure boat; hence its name. Its water is nearly blood warm, and has a decidedly disagreeable taste, as if sal soda was plentifully dissolved in it. But the most important part, to the emigrant, who has a team with him, is, that here he must take in water, as there is none for twenty miles at least, after you leave the river, which you do in a short distance; and at that point it is obtained with immense difficulty, the bank being at least five hundred feet high. Not far from this point the road forks. To the right hand is Fort Hall and the Oregon road. To the Left is Hedspeth's cut off, or the now high road to California. We passed the Old Crater to the left, and continued along to Little Creek, where we found an Indian encampment, and finding good feed, encamped; made twenty-two miles.

July 4th

This being our Independence morning, we celebrated it by firing off all our guns before sun rise. We then, after leaving our encampment, found, for a short distance, the worst road we have yet met with — hillsides, bed of creek, and a very steep hill to descend, all of which required great care; but all of which we passed with safety. In ten miles we struck Big Creek, and passed close by an elbow of it to the right. There are plenty of trout in it, but they would not bite, or we should have had a Fourth of July dinner. Nine miles further, over good road, brought us to Black Creek, up which we drove for some distance to find a fording place, and then following down, on the opposite side, to our encampment, where grass being good, but water hardly tolerable, except to bathe in, we concluded to spend the rest of the glorious Fourth; made twenty-two miles.

July 5th

We had a great many camps near us last night, and our boys set them all agoing by firing off guns, pistols, &c., and we had a tremendous shouting and yelling till sleep closed the scene. We travelled over eight miles of tolerable road, then found a spring and creek. Two miles further brought us to another creek, which we crossed. Ten miles to another, seven to another, upon which we pitched our camp—grass and water good—road good all the way. The place in which we are encamped has earned for itself (how, I have not been able to discover,) the honorable appellation of Cash Valley; made twenty-seven miles.

July 6th

This morning, before we started, we filled our water casks, &c., not knowing how far we should have to drive without. Four miles drive brought us to a narrow ravine, or rather a gorge, with scarcely room in many places for a wagon to pass through. It continues about five miles, and ends, by descending a high mountain, the greatest down-hill we have yet had, but which we got over without difficulty—we travelled on mile after mile, after our casks were empty, in continual expectation of finding water, and I believe in twenty-two miles there is a spring, some distance from the road, on the left hand; but we did not find it—but, at last came to a good spring and creek. But little grass; so we encamped, having made but thirty miles.

July 7th

Sunday. Grass being too scarce to lay over, we concluded to travel and stop a day to rest, as soon as practicable. Four miles from our encampment, the road enters a ravine, between high mountains—narrow, but wider than yesterday. Three miles further there is an excellent spring of good water, on the left hand, and in fact, there is no lack of water at every little distance, to-day. After travelling about twenty miles, we came to a creek, which we followed seven miles; plenty of grass, water and fuel. We are still in the ravine. Road good, but very dusty; made twenty-seven miles.

July 8th

Laid by to-day to recruit ourselves and our horses. There is a great deal of sickness on the route and I am constantly amongst it. Hugh Pugh has nearly got over the Purpura, but is fast sinking under a very bad cough, and it is evidently approaching the latter stage of rapid consumption.

July 9th

Left camp early, followed the creeks two miles and crossed it, then ascended the hill. The road here strikes out over a barren plain, leaving the creek. There is no more water for fourteen miles, so we took in a pailful for each horse. The road is excellent. The Fourteen Mile Creek is called Raft Creek, which we forded. It is deep and muddy. We turned out here, there being tolerable grazing. In the space of one mile the road crosses three more creeks, which I shall call Mud Creeks, they being very muddy and bad to cross. Four miles further, we came to Raft River—a small but swift stream, and forded it. Near here the Fort Hall road joins. We continued five miles up the river and encamped at the junction of a creek. Grass and water good; made twenty-six miles.

July 10th

Last night we had a fine shower of rain, which we have not seen for a long time, and hope it will lay the dust at least for a few miles. We continued up the river for three miles, and then forded it again. There is no lack of water to-day, having passed a number of good creeks. About sixteen miles from our morning's encampment, we passed over a swampy, springy piece of ground to the right hand. At the foot of the mountain, close by, there is a Warm Spring. Four miles further, the road enters between two high mountains immediately after which the most wild and romantic scenery presents itself to the eye. Rocks upon rocks, naked and piled up in the most fantastic shapes that can be imagined, are seen extending in every direction. It is called Castle City, or Steeple Rock. Understanding by the guide we had with us that there was no grass for twelve miles from this point, encamped on a small creek—grass tolerable; made twenty-two miles.

July 11th

Two miles from our morning's encampment, we emerged from Castle City, by what might truly be called its gateway, viz: a small and narrow place in the rocks, leaving just convenient space for a wagon to pass through. Three miles further on, we struck the junction of the Salt Lake road so now all the roads are again in one. Seven miles further is Steep Creek, and six miles further Birch Creek, at the foot of a mountian down which the emigrants of last year had to let their wagons with ropes; but we had no such difficulty. Two miles beyond is Goose Creek, a stream of water ten or twelve feet wide, up which we travelled five or six miles and encamped—grass, water, and fuel, plenty. The latter part of the road to-day has been very hilly, and I think the country is the wildest we have seen; made twenty-five miles.

July 12th

Fourteen miles travel this morning, up the creek, brought us to where the road leaves it, or rather, it leaves the road, and there being good grass, we turned out to feed, not knowing precisely when an opportunity might again occur. The road then passes up a branch of Goose Creek, and in three miles enters a mountain gorge, where we were led to believe we should meet with some of the almost impassable places; but to our comfort, we did not find them. We travelled up the branch of the creek three miles, crossing it twice; and at the last ford took in water, there being none for fifteen miles. We continued for eight miles further, and finding tolerable grass amongst the sage bushes, encamped; having made twenty-eight miles.

July 13th

Five miles from our morning's encampment, we entered Cold Spring Valley, near the entrance of which is a small creek. Five miles further is Cold Spring, about five rods to the left of the road—water excellent. There are also some mineral, as well as dangerous ones in this valley. About three miles beyond this, the road passes over some low hills into Thousand Spring Valley. We continued along some distance, and finding tolerable feed, turned out to noon, on Cold Creek. There is an immense number of springs in this valley—thereby its name—some cold and good, others cold and bad, and others warm, or, in fact, hot. The road continues up the valley. To-day, made thirty miles.

July 14th

Sunday. Concluded to travel to-day, and lay by to rest when we reach the Humboldt. We continued up Thousand Spring Valley eleven miles, when it terminates by a noble spring, being the last water we shall meet with, for the second time, running eastward. The road here enters a ravine, between two mountains. In seven miles we came to water—the head of some small creek which empties into the Humboldt, and in six more, struck the head of Kanyon Creek, which is also a tributary of the Humboldt. We continued down it some distance, and finding good feed, encamped; having made twenty-six miles.

July 15th

Got an early start this morning, (five o'clock,) determined to reach the Humboldt, or St. Mary's river, to-day; Kanyon Creek extends along our route all day, occasionally touching it sufficiently to furnish us most of the time with good water. A tolerable day's drive brought us at last to the long wished for stream, or, rather, one of its main branches, which is a good stream, having a broad valley well supplied with everything necessary; made twenty-seven miles.

July 16th

Laid over to rest ourselves and horses, preparatory to travelling the length of the river without another rest, as well as pushing all we can on account of scarcity of provisions, every wagon of us not having laid in a sufficient quantity, chiefly on account of false reports, from almost every one, of the distance. We having travelled about as far already, as we understood would take us to the Mines, and have, as yet, full five hundred miles to go. But I hope all who read this will take warning, as the suffering, I am sure, will be great with the late emigration, on account of grass being for the greater part eaten up. They must, of necessity, be much slower in their movements. At the end of my Daily Journal I will give a list of every thing absolutely necessary for the trip per man, as well as such other advice as we all needed. Some are now, and have been, for many days, entirely out of provisions; and the price asked by those who have, or think they have, an overplus, is really astonishing — one dollar per pound for flour, and others are even asking two dollars; bacon sixty cents, and every thing else in proportion; but the fact is, there is a general scarcity. We saw some men who were packing through on horses or mules, let animals and all their clothing go for as little food as possible, to take them though on foot. This, of itself, is sufficient to show the state of things that exists; and, I am afraid it will be much worse before we get through. Our horses are all good, and our hopes and sanguine that, with good luck, or rather with good management, as I am not much of a believer in luck, all may yet be well. So far, we have not had a single mischance in any respect; and, if the valley of the Humboldt will continue half as good as it is at the entrance, we shall have but little to fear.

July 17th

This morning we set out in fine spirits from the west side of the river, having forded it (ford good) on Monday evening. There is nothing worthy of notice, except that we passed the grave of a young man named Samuel Oliver, from Waukegan, Illinois, who was shot by an Indian, while on guard. Twenty-five miles travel brought us to the other tributary of the Humboldt, both of which, united some distance below, form the main stream—ford also good. We followed it down, occasionally leaving it for some distance, and encamped on it. Grass, wood, and water good all the way; made thirty-one miles.

July 18th

Our road to-day continues along the river valley without any change for twenty miles, when the river enters a Kanyon, in the mountains; and, the road, to avoid it, has to pass over. The old road, I believe, follows the stream, fording it a number of times, to avoid which a new track has been taken. Rumor says we shall have to go from fifteen to twenty-five miles without water; so we have encamped early to-night, and to-morrow haul up the mountain with our water casks well stored, for the weather is very hot, and roads insufferably dusty; made tweny miles.

July 19th

Three miles from our morning's encampment we filled our casks and canteens; and, leaving the river, ascended the mountain, and in eleven miles came to an excellent creek, with all our water with us, just about the time we had concluded to stop and water out of our casks. There is no necessity to take in water here, at all. We hauled the additional weight of ten pails full for nothing. The road continues down the creek some distance and crossing it, follows the river until it comes to another creek, which we forded. And, from this point there is no place, immediately near the road, fit for an encampment for twenty-seven miles. We followed the road about three miles, and turning to the left, went down to the river about two miles and found splendid grass, fuel, water, and fishing—several large Salmon Trout being caught in the camp; made twenty-six miles.

July 20th

We took in water to-day, not knowing, with any degree of certainty, how far we should have to travel without meeting with any. Sixteen miles from the creek last mentioned, we found two beautiful springs, one on each side of the road, nearly opposite each other, which form a small creek. A small quantity of water for each horse is perhaps necessary here, but can be dispensed with. There is no feed on the way, so we cut grass and hauled along for noon. About eleven miles further the road again goes down to the river, where we encamped, having to send our horses across with a strong guard. Hugh Pugh, who has, to the astonishment of us all, been some time improving, sat up and had supper with us this evening. He is dreadfully emaciated, so much so, that any one of us can carry him in our arms like a child. His cough is much better, and he promises to be as strong as ever by the time we arrive at our destination. Homeopathy has achieved such a triumph in his case as has been seldom witnessed in the practice of medicine; made twenty-five miles.

July 21st
Sunday. We concluded to travel to-day, being anxious to terminate our journey as soon as possible, and understanding that a seventeen mile stretch lay before us without water, after consultation, being deceived so frequently before, we concluded not to carry any—so started, and in nine miles again struck the river. The road here continues along the valley the remainder of the day, without our having any trouble about water. We encamped to-night in a good place for grass, but poor for water and fuel, near the side of the road, about three miles from the river. Two of our wagons, the control of which belonged to Barton & Co., got behind to-day, and failing to come up to-night, one of their men (F. Utley) stayed in camp with us all night; made twenty-seven miles.

July 22nd
Six miles from camp the road comes close to the river and passes over Rocky Point, a very rough and stony place. Water ought, by all means, to be taken in here, for the want of which we had thirty miles travel of suffering for ourselves and horses; which, had we possessed a proper guide, might have been wholly avoided. The day was equal to our hottest in Wisconsin; and, the dust—! no person can have the least idea, by a written description—it certainly is intolerable—but that does not half express my meaning—we eat it, drink it, and breathe it, night and day, the

atmosphere being loaded with it. It affects some people's eyes—but everybody has horribly sore lips—in fact, that is the great bane of the route. To-day mine became as hard as wood, there not being sufficient moisture in the body to keep them soft. The wagons are yet behind. F. Utley stayed this morning in search of them. Our drive, to-day, has been much more severe than any previous, and has been hard upon the horses. We certainly travelled as much as five miles in search of water, besides making at least thirty miles of our journey.

July 23rd

Our camp, last night, was anything but agreeable; the grass all having to be mown in a swamp, knee deep with water, and then packed half a mile to the horses. But what is there that human nature, in the shape of a parcel of California boys, cannot accomplish. It is over, and with the exception of seeing the final departure of about half a dozen horses belonging to strangers, it is well over. Two miles of travel brought us to our lost wagons. They had been travelling all night for two nights, and had consequently missed Utley, who had stayed behind. We have placed notices on the road, and made a short drive to-day, in hopes that he may catch up. The road leaves the river, where we met with Barton's wagons, and returns to it again in fourteen miles. Here the same ceremony, with regard to grass, as last evening, had to be repeated, only that the half mile was a whole one. To-night it was far worse than ever—we being under the necessity of encamping on the bare dust, by the bank of the river, and obliged to swim over to mow grass for the horses, and haul it across with ropes—and could not get more than one-fourth sufficient at that—so that our poor horses had indeed to go hungry. Barton, on account of having driven last night, had to stay behind and rest teams—and, to the astonishment of us all, drove past us this evening, intending to drive all night, with Utley still behind. Some of our men do not hesitate to say he is doing it intentionally. He has, most certainly, frequently expressed an opinion against night travelling. Utley may be ahead, or if behind, may possibly get in with some one else. But his fate is uncertain, and we are all in suspense. About two miles before we encamped, we passed where the road turns to the right, and is called Lawson's Route. It must by no means be taken; all that is necessary to avoid it is to follow the course of the river, and all will be well; made seventeen miles.

July 24th

Started early this morning determined to find a place where we could rest our horses, as well as wait a day for Utley, should he be behind. After three miles drive we met with good feed and encamped, but have not seen or heard of Utley. The wagon that was travelling with us from Michigan City, had a horse laid down yesterday, and refused to go any further; so they stayed behind and expect again to rejoin us before to-morrow morning, as they had five horses and now have but three of them; made three miles.

July 25th

Started off with our horses as good as new this morning, with a bag full of grass for each horse, in case we should fail, at noon or night, to find any. Nine miles from the camp the road leaves the river. Here we took in six pails of water, and commenced to cross the mountains; six miles of drive brought us again to the river, to that our water was useless. Here there being no grass, we gave our horses some that we had brought along. When we had been here about half an hour, up came Utley, driving a two-horse team. Glad enough to see him safe. He had walked backwards and forwards in vain, looking for Barton, all the day we left him, without being able to get anything to eat until nine o'clock at night, when coming up to a wagon from Walworth County, Wisconsin, belonging to two brothers of the name of Askens, they took him in and treated him in the kindest manner. Being short of provisions themselves, they invited him to share with them, telling him he should not starve as long as they had any thing to eat. There are yet some sunny spots in human nature. He will now continue amongst us until we overtake Barton, which we shall undoubtedly do, night travelling being more severe on horses. The road from here continues along the valley of the river the rest of the day. Finding good grass, by swimming the river, we encamped. The Michigan City wagon has not yet come up; made twenty-six miles.

July 26th

To-day the road continues along the river valley. Some distance from camp it takes quite a turn to avoid a creek and marsh, and after fording the creek, passes over the bluffs for about two miles — road very rough and stony. It then comes again to the river. The rest of the distance to-day has been heavy sand. There is quite a dispute, or rather a speculation, as to the distance to the Sink — the difference varying from twenty to eighty miles. I suppose we shall all know when we get there, that being the confines of the desert. At all events, we encamped early, at a convenient place for cutting grass, but had to swim the river for it; so we have laid in our stock of hay, preparatory to crossing it, and intend to take in water at the last convenient place where it is fit for use. At the Sink itself, it is unfit for man or beast; made twenty-two miles.

July 27th

Started this morning, looking still for the Desert, but although we have seen three or four men who were through last year, they either all differ, or can give no correct information. The road to-day is very heavy indeed, and I am afraid will wear hard upon our teams; but we have got to get through the sand and back to our old kind of going, viz: dust about six inches deep, and light as feathers; we drove about three miles though it and encamped; making twenty miles.

July 28th

This morning our spirits were rather dampened, one horse, belonging to Peter Port & Company, had to be left behind, and yesterday's drive has made havoc among all of them; one mile from our camp the road leaves the river and ascends a very heavy sand hill, but it is short. Before leaving the river, about a pail full of water for each horse ought to be taken in, as it is sixteen miles before you again reach the river. There has been a good deal of stony road in the early part of the day. After striking the river, the road continues along near it. At our encampment, to-night, there is no grass to be found, and we are feeding the hay prepared for the Desert. The Sink, or Humboldt Lake, is not yet found, and appears to be getting further off — at least if tales are to be noticed; made twenty-two miles.

July 29th

Five miles from our morning's encampment we found some grass over the river, and stopped to cut it and feed our horses, as well as carry what we could with us. The road continues along the valley of the river, but all around us begins to assume a more barren appearance. We looked in vain for grass to-night, and had again to feed out our hay intended for the desert. The Sink, about which I have heard as much said, the last five or six days, as about a Presidential Election, is yet in the distance, but we are assured it is only ten miles off; and, in fact, two of our company's wagons have drove on to it, or at least made the attempt; made twenty-four miles.

July 30th

We started this morning at three o'clock, intending to arrive early at the Sink. Nine miles drive brought us again to the river, through a deep ravine, and there we found Barton & Company. Utley and he have made a compromise, and he goes in his wagon. There was no feed but willows at this point, and a great many camps were using them. We watered, and turning our faces westward, were, as soon as matters were adjusted with all parties, again on our journey. To-day the much talked of Sink is still in the distance, and to-night our horses have to make their first attempt at feasting on willows; made twenty-two miles.

July 31st

Started early, having pretty good confidence that a drive of twenty miles would bring us to the "Big Slough," but in case of failure, three of us followed the river — a resort I would not advise any one to undertake for the future, on foot; Fleming, Lytle, and myself, after walking fifteen miles, met the teams but an impassable slough lay between us, which took hard

upon twenty miles to walk round—rather severe, after a four o'clock breakfast, with not a morsel of food with us. In the evening we reached the **Big
Slough**, and the first camp we came to the pangs of hunger emboldened me
to inquire if a meal of any thing could be got on any terms; but, although a
quantity of bread was baked and lay exposed to our view, as if to provoke
our appetites to desperation, (for it was such bread as we have not tasted for
three weeks,) we met with a denial; they, or in fact, scarcely any body else,
not having more than five or six days provisions on hand. At length, our
wagons not being anywhere to be found, I made another attempt at a
wagon where there was one of the tender sex, and there we succeeded in
getting some good bread—all they had cooked. These we considered
human folks. A rest, and another short walk brought us to the **wagons.**
They had arrived at twelve o'clock M., and had cut any quantity of hay for
the Desert, the third time. This time we are right—and let none be
deceived after this. I can assure them the Humboldt River is every mile I
have estimated it at; and they need not fear in the least of getting on the
Desert without knowing it. The road forks, and the left hand turns to the
Big Slough, where there is good grass enough for all, and plenty to spare.
Straight ahead will take you to the Desert—distance twenty miles. At the
Forks there is a large, peculiar shaped, isolated mountain, or rather a
double mound; one with a large base, with a smaller one on the top of it.
This mountain is different in shape from any thing else I have seen on
the Humboldt. Whoever may be furnished with this, as a guide, may rest
assured till they see this object, as well as the termination of the mountain
ranges ahead, that their course is still onward, no matter what you may hear
other people say. The road may, and doubtless will, differ a little from
year to year, but the leading features will still be the same. Sixteen miles
ahead are some Sulphur Springs, the last water we get on this side of the
Desert. The Humboldt River is so far the hardest part of the route for both
man and beast—in fact, the whole route is the most destructive one that
can be imagined. Wagons, harness, and all other kinds of stock, are

strewed all along the way; as to the live stock, or rather that which left home alive, is incredible. Horses, mules, and oxen, lay indiscriminately on the road side, putrifying, and rendering the air pestilential — and this is the early part of the emigration. Thousands are behind us; what may be their fate, it is uncertain to prognosticate. I should not like to be the last — the first is bad enough. We made twenty miles of our journey to-day.

August 1st

To-day we laid by to rest ourselves and horses — a thing much needed by both, as probably a drive of eighty miles is before us, without an opportunity of more than a three hour's feed at a time, until the desert is crossed. At half-past five in the evening, three wagons were ready for a start. We did not like to leave the rest behind, but necessity compelled. We had scarcely provisions sufficient to last across. Being well loaded with hay, we drove fifteen miles, and no knowing where we were, and wishing to find the Sulphur Springs, we rounded to for an encampment, fed our horses, set our guard, and went to sleep; having made fifteen miles.

August 2nd

At sunrise we were again on the road, and discovered we were near where the river widens considerably, and forms what has been called Humboldt Lake; but though the stream is much higher than has ever been known at this season, it is not worthy the name of Lake. The country all around presents a dreary and barren appearance. The Sulphur Springs are overflown on account of high water, but the river itself is fit for use in consequence. The water of this region appears to be strongly impregnated with nitre; it acts as a powerful diuretic, and is in consequence exceedingly debilitating. We drove ten miles, and filling our casks, canteens, &c., where other people were doing the same, had even eight miles further to go before we got to the Desert proper, or rather before we entirely leave water. Here we arrived at 2 o'clock, and stopped to rest and feed after fording, for a small stream runs further still. This is, I suppose, what has been called the Sink, but has quite a different appearance to what I expected. It consists of a series of sloughs which generally terminate near this spot, but the one we forded passes with a strong current, how far I know not. I am told they all extend much further than they have been known to do before. At half-past four we harnessed and started; road tolerably good for several miles. We drove six hours, and stopped to feed two hours, and then started again. Two miles brought us to a belt of heavy sand. Here the wagons were left in large quantities, some burning and many partly burned. We continued along, occasionally crossing these belts of sand, all of which were exceedingly heavy. After a five hours' drive, we again stopped and fed; this was about sunrise. Here we stayed three hours, and by this time it was growing pretty hot; we soon after this struck the heavy sand which we expected to find at the other end of the route. Here, our water being gone, we threw away our casks, tents, buffalo robes, and many other things to lighten our load; we toiled on through the sand and heat, until we got within five miles of Pilot river; here we understood there was a spring of good water, by the side of a small lake of salt water, on the top of a hill, about three miles from the river, on the left hand, and within three miles of us; so we took our horses out of the harness and led them to the spring, which we easily found. On getting to the top of the hill, a small lake ushers itself into view, five or six hundred feet below you. A rather steep descent took us to the bottom, down which we succeeded in getting our horses; here, immediately at the bottom is one of the most beautiful springs I have ever seen, of most excellent water. Oh! how sweet and delicious is a draught of good cold water when you are suffering with burning thirst. We drank carefully and let our horses do the same, staying about an hour at the spring. I drank in that hour at least a gallon. We returned to our wagons, ate up the last morsel of provisions we had, except two quarts of corn meal, that we succeeded in buying from a wagon on the Desert, at $1 per quart; we then started again, and at dark succeeded in reaching the river. Here we found quite a trading post; flour a dollar and a half a pound, and everything else in proportion; we went supperless to bed, after buying two dollars worth of hay for our horses.

August 3rd

Early in the morning we were up and off four miles up the river, where there is good feed for the horses; here we found another trading post; prices about the same. We bought a fat cow for fifty dollars, and after killing and reserving enough for ourselves for the remainder of the journey, had no difficulty in selling the rest at twenty-five and thirty cents per pound, by which move we nearly got our own supply clear. The Desert and its effects upon the emigration is worthy of particular notice. It would not be as bad as it is, did it not follow close after the Humboldt river, the water of which has such a weakening influence on the stock, that it is next to a miracle to get over safe without leaving some, if not all of them, behind. The scene witnessed beggars description; it is wholly impossible to convey the least idea to the mind of any one who has never beheld such a sickening aspect. Hundreds—I might almost say thousands—of dead and dying animals, scattered around, chiefly horses; they appear to suffer more than either mules or oxen, but oxen are decidedly the best for the journey. We have succeeded thus far in keeping all our horses, a circumstance I believe without a parallel. There was water for sale on the Desert, seven or eight miles from the river, at only fifty cents per quart, which of course we did not buy at that price. One, if not more of the wagons are going to peddle the precious fluid. The distance across the Desert is called forty miles; it is that, at least; I should call it forty-five. To-day was my birthday, and I think I need hardly say it was the hardest day of my life. It will be seen that we had to carry hay eighty miles from the Big Slough to Carson, or Pilot river.

August 4th

Today, being Sunday, we made it as much a day of rest as possible, but had to sell our beef, cook some provisions, and attend to other little matters.

August 5th

Several of us are preparing to pack through on foot, in order to hasten along, and make less provisions do, as well as relieve our teams, and prepare a location. Our knapsacks and provisions are all ready for an early start in the morning.

August 6th

This morning, at sunrise twelve of us, having provisions cooked for three days, started with our packs on our backs, viz: Hamilton, and myself from our wagon, Fleming and Waldron from Bennett's, Bumps and Wallace from Port's, Rice and Dutch John from Barton's, Smith and Talcott from Fratt's, and Gibson and Gilson from Devin's, a wagon that had previously joined us from Iowa, that Gibson was travelling in, all of us from Racine, except Gibson, who was from Iowa. We took the road that follows the river for five miles, it then leaves the river for sixteen miles, over a desert without a drop of water or any grass. We took a path that led down the river all the way, and after enjoying the cool shade of Cottonwood trees through the heat of the day, we finished our day's work. Two miles, after having regained the road, we encamped in the open air, with one blanket to cover each of us, cutting some willows to rest our weary bodies on, in lieu of a feather bed, and quietly went to sleep, having made twenty-three miles.

August 7th

A half-past twelve we were stirring again. A desert of twenty-six miles was stretched out before us, and had to be performed without the benefit of a single shade tree, and consequently without a rest. We thought it best to take it in the cool of the morning, there not being a drop of water in the whole distance and the road, with the exception of four miles, very heavy sand. There is also no grass for animals, which, in our situation, did not at all affect us. We filled our canteens and started at half-past twelve o'clock. At half-past three we stopped and got breakfast, and at ten arrived again at the river, after a severe walk. Here we are, once more under the welcome shade. After regaling ourselves with ready baked bread, at one dollar and a half per pound, and got pretty well rested. At four o'clock we again set out, and followed the wagon road along the river seven miles, and encamped, having made thirty-three miles.

August 8th

Started at sunrise—in about one mile the road leaves the river and does not return to it again in twelve miles. It is hilly, sandy, and stoney, very bad for wagons, and in fact they are behind, and men, horses, mules, and oxen are packed without discrimination. It is even amusing to see the change. I believe the foot packers have the best of the bargain, as they have no animals to take care of. We hear continually of gold digging being successfully carried on this side of the mountains. But as it is always some distance from the road, we have not yet been to see. About every ten miles there is a Trading Post, and it is to their interest, if possible, to induce the traveller to remain and pay their enormous prices. The road, for the rest of the day, occasionally touches the river, so that there is no scarcity of water, and the grass is excellent. We travelled along from half-past two till seven, and encamped by a trading post; having made twenty-seven miles.

August 9th

Last night was so intolerably cold that we could not sleep, our encampment being at the foot of Sierra Nevada Mountains. At half-past twelve we were all up, and again on our route to keep our blood in circulation. We walked seven miles and came to the Mormon Station, beautifully situated in a grove of immense pines. Here we made a good fire and cooked breakfast, rested awhile, and then moved along. The road continues along the foot of the mountain. About two miles further on there is a quantity of Hot Springs, immediately on the left of the road, or in fact, coming out of the road itself. There is all the way to-day, a broad and beautiful valley, well supplied with grass of all kinds—by far the best we have seen. The road, too, is good for wagons—and beautiful mountain creeks, with water cold as ice and clear as crystal, occurring every now and then. The mountain side is covered to the very top with very large and stately pine timber, altogether, having a very fine appearance. After a walk of fourteen miles, we rested under the welcome shade of an immense pine, with a cotton-wood grove close by on the left, and a delicous stream of water, gently meandering through it, and regaled ourselves with a cup of excellent coffee. Snow frequently occurs on the tops of the mountains, although the heat is really oppressive immediately below. There is some of the finest scenery here to be witnessed that has occurred on our whole route, and the best of all our long and toilsóme journey is fast drawing to a close. The first settlement being within about one hundred miles of us. After our rest, we proceeded, and in about nine miles the valley abruptly terminates by a mountain range, and the river comes boiling and leaping out of a large kanyon or gap, hewn through the mountain by some violent convulsion of old Dame Nature. We encamped at the mouth, having made, in all, thirty miles.

August 10th

This morning, early, we entered the kanyon, up which the road passes. It is, or at least appears to be, almost impassable for wagons. The road crosses the river, which is all along a roaring torrent, three times; but, at each crossing there is a tolerable log bridge. The kanyon is six miles long, and all through the scenery is grand and imposing. One mile further on, we found a trading post, where we bought and cooked some provisions. We then proceeded eleven miles, through valleys and over hills, grass being good in many places, until we came to the foot of the first steep mountain. One of our party (Waldron) having been sick all day, and scarcely able to travel, Fleming and myself stayed here with him, and the rest of the party crossed the mountain to the next trading post—so that this will hereafter be a history of the travels of three of us alone; made eighteen miles.

August 11th

Sunday. Laying by was out of the question, and Waldron being some better, and able to travel slowly, at six o'clock we began to ascend the mountain—about one mile of steep ascent brought us to the summit, where are two small lakes, one on each side of the road. Five miles of gradual descent brought us to the next trading post, where we got flour for seventy-five cents per pound. We bought but little, having the highest and last ascent directly before us; towards this we proceeded, and after a hard climb of five miles, once more gained the summit, and stood upon the top of the Sierra Nevada, or Snowy Mountains, the highest point on our whole route. I think but few wagons can ever cross this place; the snow, in some places, is more than thirty feet deep in the road; but some have already gone over. After proceeding about a mile further, we halted and cooked dinner. Our road, for the rest of the day, is mountainous—but for the most part descending. Twelve miles brought us to the next trading post, where we encamped, Waldron tired enough, having walked twenty-four miles over the most mountainous road in the world.

August 12th

After a walk of five miles this morning, we found a grogshop on the road-side kept by two brothers of the name of Hulbert, from Rochester, Racine County. They started on the 21st of March, had beat us a month, and had returned fifty-five miles three weeks ago, and since been trading where they now are, in provisions of all kinds, and liquors. They were out of most kinds of eatables, but had plenty of drink. They were located within half a mile of Tragedy Springs, (so called from three emigrants being shot by the Indians, last year, whilst in their tent.) Here we rested awhile, and proceeded—all around us, as far as the eye can reach, are mountains covered with pine of various kinds, some of them very large. Compared with what we have passed over; the road is tolerable—rather uneven, but for the most part descending. We are at present taking our dinners by the side of a good spring, one hundred and fifty yards to the left of the road, six miles from Tragedy Springs. Four miles further brought us to Leek Valley and Springs, where there is a trading post, excellent water, and good grass, some distance down the valley. We bought some beef and bread here, and went two miles further; where, finding an excellent spring fifty yards to the left of the road, we encamped; having made eighteen miles.

August 13th

This morning we again set out on our weary journey with a light breakfast—money getting rather scarce. We had to go ten miles to the next station—road uneven, and water scarce—none between our camp and the station. We arrived there and found all sorts of provisions sold out; and, hungry enough, we proceeded to the next, six miles off. But my lucky star was in the ascendent; one mile further, I discovered some packers, like ourselves, dining, and succeeded in getting one pound of flour of them, for which I paid a dollar, which we immediately baked into cakes, and barely satisfied the cravings of hunger. In the midst of dinner we were surprised by the appearance of Wright, Thorpe, and Quin, whom we left at the Desert. They started with two horses and a light wagon, the day after us, and soon after sold their horses, &c., for eighty dollars, and are packing it through like ourselves. We think they have done well; but they had no choice—to sell or starve—as begging was out of the question so long as they had a team. Water begins to be more seldom met with. Occasionally we have to go eight or ten miles without it; and when found, it is some distance from the road, down deep ravines—the road itself, running for the most part on high ridges. We left a creek here, and had no more until our arrival at the next station, eight miles, where there is a spring and creek of excellent water in a ravine, studded with the most magnificnt pines in the world—many with trunks being at least ten feet in diameter at the base, and towering to an immense height. We measured a fallen one, not by any means one of the largest, and found it to be one hundred and eighty-six feet long, although the top was broken off at upwards of twelve inches in diameter, and it was four feet at the base. They generally run up as straight as arrows, and have small branches, in most cases, down to the bottom. We made to-day, eighteen miles.

August 14th

Our party now consists of five; one (Thorpe) being tired, stopped to rest and has not yet come up with us. After an early breakfast we again set out; the road heavy, the dust being very deep, with countless numbers of loose stones, which, combined with continued up-hill and down-hill, makes travelling pretty hard business, but we hope by to-morrow noon to close the drama. Yesterday and to-day oak has occasionally made its appearance amongst the pine, and I had almost forgot to notice the white cedar; it rivals the pine, but is not so plentiful, and I doubt not it could cut a good figure by the side of "even the tall cedars of Lebanon," so famous in Scripture. Nine miles brought us to another station, where, as well as last night, we bought flour for 50 cents per pound; so that some advantage accrues from our proximity to the diggings. Here, water being nearer the road than again for 15 miles, or at least they tell us so, we stopped and cooked our dinners; a walk of six miles brought us to the forks of the road, the right hand leading to Hangtown, or Placerville, and the left to Weberville, the right being the best, and there being but little if any difference in the distance, we steered for Placerville, (it was formerly called Hangtown on account of Judge Lynch having more than once, I believe, paid it a visit). Half a mile beyond the Forks, we found a spring of good water, and being told there was no more for ten miles, we turned about fifty yards to the right hand and encamped, having made fifteen miles.

James S. Shepherd

Early in the morning we got breakfast, and were off again; but Quin being attacked with diarrhea in the night, could make but slow progress. In two or three miles Wright picked up an old horse which had been worn out and left by some one; Quin got on and rode to Johnson's Ranche, thirteen miles, and there sold him for ten dollars. Being only six miles from Placerville, we got flour for twenty-two cents, and other things in proportion, and went under the shade and cooked our dinners. Here is a house and farm, some evidence of civilization; rather rough but welcome to the eyes of men who had roamed in the wilderness as long as we had, it being the first we had seen since leaving Fort Laramie, a distance of nearly two thousand miles, and the whole country between a mountainous and barren waste, except along the river valleys; here also, the gold diggings commence. We did not go to see the first one in operation, it being some distance from the road, but in a walk of three miles we began to see them in full operation, in a small creek, in a ravine, which runs through Placerville; but water is at present rather scarce, so that they are confined to the bed of the creek, but the small ravines which put into it, and are full of water in the rainy season, are said to be much richer, but not available at present. We stayed some little time and watched the miners at work; it looks like small business, but the result is the pure stuff, almost as much so as it can be made, it being washed and hammered by friction with the rocks and loose stones it is found amongst in its passage from the mountains, until it is (whatever may be its original condition, which does not seem to be at all known here,) reduced to small lumps, scales and grains, and may be termed grain gold. At Placerville, we got flour for eighteen cents, and pork for twenty-five cents; so that living in the mines is not so very expensive after all. But our great object is accomplished—our long and weary journey is at an end, and California is reached in safety. We encamped as usual in the open air, our finances not allowing any greater luxury at present, and enjoyed a good night's repose; having made nineteen miles.

After breakfast, we walked into town to look around and ascertain what sort of a place we were in, or rather, what sort of a place a California village could be. The creek and ravine before mentioned runs through the centre of the place, or in fact the village is built in the ravine, which is dug up in all directions, giving the place the roughest appearance ever beheld. It is entirely new, and built up with all kinds of shanties, from a tent made of bushes, to a tolerable frame building. The Empire Hotel, a public gambling house, is a large and good frame building, the best in the place. Gambling is carried on here to a great extent, in open sight, in the bar-rooms, which are large and filled with gaming tables; it seems to be as much a business as gold digging. Some little distance further I saw the office and sign of Dr. Ruddock, who came out from Southport last year; I hunted him up, and we had a long conversation. Homeopathy, he says, is quite popular in California, but few to practice it, and those few are doing well. I paid one dollar for getting my boot heels pieced, which the shoemaker did in about half an hour. New boots are from sixteen to twenty-four dollars per pair. We heard of some of our company who had arrived before, being down the creek, mining; so down we went to look for them. We found some of them at work, and after dining with them, went to work to help them. Fleming with Rice, whose companion was sick, and myself with Gilson and Gibson, so that my mining commenced on a Friday, generally considered my lucky day. We worked three hours, and took out three dollars and three bits, or York shillings. This is but little, but if a miner makes five dollars a day he is doing well, and it will cost him one dollar a day for board. I got three patients to-day, but it must certainly be a healthy country; every one who has been here a year, says the climate is a splendid one. We shall most likely stay here until the teams arrive and Waldron gets recruited. Wright, Thorpe and Quin have obtained tools, and are going to work tomorrow morning on the creek. A set of tools sufficient for two, three, or four men, as the diggings happens to be, will cost at least fifty dollars; they consist of a pick-axe, shovel, rocker, pail, and pan, and are all of them indispensable, even if a man works alone.

August 17th

To-day we were inclined to be lazy, and consequently did not do much. I got some patients, and Fleming and myself borrowed some mining tools of Dr. Ruddock, and went prospecting, that is, looking for a place to dig, but had no success; so at night, returned the tools, but have arrived at no conclusion at present.

Sunday. Placerville is thronged with miners, the stores are all open, as well as the gambling houses, and the Lord's Day is the greatest day for business of the whole week. I am in the office with Dr. Ruddock, assisting him, diarrhea and dysentery being very prevalent. On one side is a building framed with poles, over which cloth is stretched, and inside is a Methodist Preacher expounding the Word of God at the top of his voice; whilst on the other hand is an auctioneer selling horses, in equally as high a tone. What a world is California. Fratt's and Peter Port's teams arrived to-day all safe; they report ours not far behind.

August 24th

This evening our teams arrived all safe, except a horse stolen from each of Lytle's and Bennett's wagons, about one hundred miles back in the mountains, which accident caused Bennett's wagon to be converted into a cart, they having lost one horse previously. Our boys, Lytle and Hamilton, taking all things into account, have done better than any one who left Racine; they are the only ones who have yet brought through the wagon they started with from Racine; the rest having picked up lighter ones, or gone to packing. They have also brought through five of us safe, more by one than any other wagon; and Hugh Pugh has been hauled at least half the distance, and has come in restored to comparative health, as well as all the clothing, bedding &c., belonging to us all; they have done well. Horses, &c., are low, but I hope they will get a good price.

August 25th

Our boys have sold the four horses, wagons and harness, notwithstanding it being Sunday, — which, by-the-by, I think was lucky for them, the town always being crowded on the Lord's Day—for four hundred dollars. They have done well, and are going to-morrow to where Judge Bryan is, a distance of thirty-five miles. May they continue to do well. I am located in Placerville in the practice of medicine with Dr. Ruddock.

Across the Plains to California

California, the place towards which the attention of so many is turned, is probably of all places on earth, the worst to give an opinion upon. There is no doubt of there being plenty of gold, much more than will ever be obtained by any means, and I have no doubt that mining will be carried on for years to come; but the time seems to be past when fortunes were made in a day, or rather but few such cases ever have been, and those few have been sounded all over the United States, until men have magnified them beyond all reason, and the result has been a gold fever, or mania, which I and thousands of others have proved can be easily cured by a journey overland to California. Thousands have returned who came this year, disappointed and crestfallen; but I think the majority of such cases have been as foolish in returning without due deliberation, as they were in leaving home at all; and I hesitate not to say, that with those who remain, homesickness is as prevailing an epidemic, as the gold fever was in the Western States last winter. The average price that miners can earn is probably three dollars a day, one of which it will cost him to live; and if he should be taken sick, diseases are very severe, and getting up again to a state of health very slow, almost impossible. The climate can be told in a few words; there are two seasons of the year, one rainy almost incessantly, and the other dry in the same ratio. Since I have been here it has been dry, with the exception of two showers, and the days have been very hot, and the nights very cold; the evenings are truly splendid, but the climate on the whole is not such as I like. There seems to be but little if any difference in the mines; the leading features of all are the same; some are more lucky than others, which means that the gold is not all over alike, consequently some find it, while others fail to do so; but it is obtained by great labor alone. I have given but a short description of California, but any further must only be a repetition of words. 'Tis true, I have seen but little of the country at present, but have heard a great deal, and have on that based my opinion. As I promised in my Journal of July 16, I will now proceed to give that instruction and advice to the future emigrant, which we all so much needed this season. 1st. Let your wagon be light, but strong, with a good cover; have four yoke of good oxen, five years old, have them shod, and two sets of extra shoes to carry along, with a sufficient quantity of nails to put them on; have three men and no more, under any consideration to a wagon, and have a spare horse or mule, as a saddle beast — two would be better than one. 2nd. Have four hundred pounds of provisions per man, divided as follows: one hundred lbs. of hard bread, one hundred and fifty lbs. of flour, one hundred lbs. of bacon, 25 lbs. of sugar, and some rice, tea or coffee, beans, and dried fruit, to make up the remainder; one gallon of vinegar per man is indispensable, and some tartaric acid, and one small keg of butter per wagon will be a luxury not easily dispensed with. Bring no mining tools with you, nor any new improvements that any one may profess to have discovered in that line; I have seen a great many this season, but they are all useless here. Always keep this maxim before your eyes, that it is worth at least dollars a pound to bring anything over the Plains. Bring good bedding, at least two good woolen blankets, as the nights are so cold the greater part of the route. Let your clothing be good and substantial, with woolen shirts and drawers, but no more outer garments than you want on the road, as clothing is nearly as cheap here as in the States; in other words, let your load be as light as possible. Start from home so that you can leave the frontier about the middle of April; never mind what people say about there being no grass, but load down with grain, and put out; grass had better be scarce at first, than at the last end of the journey. But above all, do not load down with guns and ammunition; one good rifle to each wagon, and a revolver for each man, is quite sufficient; three-fourths of the fire arms were thrown away this season. If these rules are strictly followed, there may be some chance of getting through safe, wagon and all; if not, the same disastrous events will take place that have this year, viz: disappointment, starvation, and death in the most frightful forms. Another thing must be no means be forgot; it was generally supposed this year, that after we left the frontier, money was of no use; it is the greatest mistake possible; I know of no part of the world where money is of more use than in crossing the Plains, and where a man is more helpless without it. No man ought to leave home without at least two hundred dollars. I would also earnestly advise all those, let their inclination be ever so strongly to come, who are over forty years of age, to stay at home, as they will in all probability, after once leaving it for this perilous journey and country, never return.

The distance from Racine to Fort Leavenworth, the point from which we started, or any other on the frontier will be about the same, is not far from five hundred and fifty miles; and in summing it up, I find my estimates make the distance from there to Placerville, two thousand one hundred and forty-one miles; thus making the whole distance from Racine, Wisconsin, to Placerville, California, two thousand, six hundred and ninety-one miles. Sacramento City is fifty miles west of Placerville.

The James S. Shepherd, JOURNAL OF TRAVEL ACROSS THE PLAINS TO CALIFORNIA AND GUIDE TO THE FUTURE EMIGRANT *is one of the rarest titles pertaining to the American West, with two known original copies, one of which has disappeared. The only known original is now in the Huntington Library at San Marino, California. This could be the George Langlois copy, by use of which a small edition was printed nearly half a century ago, probably at Placerville, California. Howes states that the edition was 250 copies but Mr. Langlois told me 200 copies. The sheets were printed in two colors at Ye Galleon Press in 1978, now sixteen years back in the dusty past. The copies were not bound because some sheets were printed out of register. The material surfaced recently in the Ye Galleon book store room and a sad decision was made to bind them as they were. There would have been some difficulty matching the heavy paper stock. The press offers its apology for the misregister. The pages were set in the 1970's by Dale LaTendresse, and were printed on a Hamada duplicator Model 770. Finishing printing was done in 1994 by Garry Adams using a Chief 17 duplicator. The hard case binding is by Arts and Crafts Book Manufacturing Company, Oakesdale, Washington, Al and Melissa Chidester.*